melanie walsh

my flower,
your flower

eden project

Carrots grow hidden in

the dark under ground.

Cherries grow
in the sunshine,
hanging on trees.
But . . .

yum yum, they both
taste delicious.

Cactuses
live in the
hot, dry
desert.

Stinging nettles live
in rainy fields, but . . .

ouch, they can both hurt your skin!

Bluebells come
from bulbs

and grow wild in
the woods.

Pinks come from seeds and grow in gardens, but . . .

they both smell
wonderful, ah!

Clover plants are small

and grow under your feet.

Oak trees are huge and reach high into the sky. But . . . .

look, they both
have pretty leaves.

Leaves go
crunch, crunch
on autumn days.

Branches swish and creak in winter winds. But . . .

shhh,
everything is
peaceful

on lazy
summer
afternoons.

The Eden Project brings plants and people together.
It is dedicated to developing a greater understanding
of our shared global garden, encouraging us to
respect plants and to protect them.

MY FLOWER, YOUR FLOWER
AN EDEN PROJECT BOOK
ISBN 978 1 905 81145 8

Published in Great Britain by Eden Project Books
an imprint of Transworld Publishers

This edition published 2004

3 5 7 9 10 8 6 4

Eden Project Books are published by Transworld Publishers
Addresses for companies within The Random House Group Limited can
be found at: www.randomhouse.co.uk/offices.htm

RANDOM HOUSE AUSTRALIA (PTY) LTD
20 Alfred Street, Milsons Point, Sydney,
New South Wales 2061, Australia

RANDOM HOUSE NEW ZEALAND LTD
18 Poland Road, Glenfield, Auckland 10, New Zealand

RANDOM HOUSE (PTY) LTD
Endulini, 5A Jubilee Road, Parktown 2193, South Africa

THE RANDOM HOUSE GROUP Limited Reg. No. 954009
www.kidsatrandomhouse.co.uk
www.edenproject.com

A CIP catalogue record for this book is available
from the British Library.

Printed and bound in Singapore